Editor
Jennifer Overend Prior, M. Ed.

Managing Editor
Ina Massler Levin, M.A.

Editor-in-Chief
Sharon Coan, M.S. Ed.

Illustrator
Bruce Hedges

Cover Artist
Barb Lorseyedi

Art Coordinator
Kevin Barnes

Art Director
CJae Froshay

Imaging
Ralph Olmedo, Jr.

Product Manager
Phil Garcia

Copyrighted materials and content reprinted with permission from Renaissance Corporate Services, Inc.

Publisher
Mary D. Smith, M.S. Ed.

Practice Makes Perfect
Reading Comprehension

GRADE 6

Author

Teacher Created Resources Staff

Teacher Created Resources

Teacher Created Resources, Inc.
6421 Industry Way
Westminster, CA 92683
www.teachercreated.com

ISBN 13: 978-0-7439-3367-4

©2003 Teacher Created Resources, Inc.
Reprinted, 2007
Made in U.S.A.

Table of Contents

Introduction

The old adage "practice makes perfect" can really hold true for your child and his or her education. The more practice and exposure your child has with concepts being taught in school, the more success he or she is likely to experience. For many parents, knowing how to help their children may be frustrating because the resources may not be readily available.

As a parent it is also difficult to know where to focus your efforts so that the extra practice your child receives at home supports what he or she is learning in school.

This book has been written to help parents and teachers reinforce basic skills with children. *Practice Makes Perfect: Reading Comprehension* gives practice with reading and answering questions to help students fully comprehend what is read. The exercises in this book can be done sequentially or can be taken out of order, as needed.

After reading the story, the questions can be answered either by circling the answers or by reproducing and using the fill-in answer sheets on pages 46 and 47. The practice tests, one for each of the areas of reading, can be bubbled in on the answer pages that are provided for each test.

The following standards or objectives will be met or reinforced by completing the practice pages included in this book. These standards and objectives are similar to the ones required by your state and school district. These standards and objectives are appropriate for the sixth grade.

- The student will demonstrate competence in making predictions about what is being read.
- The student will demonstrate competence in using various reading strategies to read the stories and answer the questions.
- The student will demonstrate competence in finding the main idea in a story, making inferences and making predictions.
- The student will be familiar with different types of reading (fiction, nonfiction, informational).
- The student will be able to use context clues and other aides to determine the meaning of a word.

How to Make the Most of This Book

Here are some useful ideas for making the most of this book:

- Set aside a specific place in your home to work on this book. Keep the area neat and tidy with materials ready on hand.
- Set up a certain time of day to work on these practice pages to establish consistency, or look for times in your day or week that are less hectic and conducive to practicing skills.
- Keep all practice sessions with your child positive and constructive. If the mood becomes frustrated or tense, set the book aside and look for another time to practice with your child.
- Forcing your child to perform will not help. Do not use this book as a punishment.
- Review the work your child has done.
- Pay attention to the areas in which your child has the most difficulty. Provide extra guidance and exercises in those areas.
- Read aloud with your child and ask reading comprehension questions.

Lost!

Denny and Mark had come to Sun Mountain Resort with their eighth-grade class. The first day had been great. Everyone enjoyed snowball fights and races down the slopes. The next day was very cold and no one wanted to go outside. "I'm not wasting the day inside!" Mark declared. He and Denny decided to brave the weather and try out a new ski run.

By noon the boys were bored, so they set off into the forest. At first it was great. The boys followed some wolf tracks for awhile, but when they realized they had left the path, they turned back. Before they could find the path, snow began to fall.

"This doesn't look good," Denny said. The snow seemed to fall faster, and the sun, which had been bright just a few minutes before, seemed to disappear all at once. Mark could hear fear in his friend's voice. He was scared, too. Their clothes, which had gotten wet while the boys were skiing, now offered little protection against the cold.

"We have to stay put," Denny said. "They'll figure out we're lost and come for us."

Peering up at the pine trees, Mark said, "I read a story once where someone trapped in a snowstorm made a tent from tree branches. Think it would work?"

Denny felt the snow coming down faster. "Can't hurt," he said, "but we'd better hurry."

The two worked quickly. Mark, who was taller, found a number of good-sized pine branches that were hanging low enough to pull down. Denny found a place where two tree trunks grew close together. They made a lean-to of branches and spread some of the branches on the ground underneath the shelter. Then they crawled inside.

The boys sat for what seemed like hours. It grew completely dark. The snow stopped, but an icy wind blew through the lean-to. Mark's hands and feet went numb. So did Denny's. "I don't want to die here," Mark whispered in the dark.

"We're not going to die!" Denny said. But in the back of his mind, he wasn't so sure. Before he could say anything else, he saw a flash of light. Rescuers! The boys scrambled out of their lean-to just as a crowd of people reached them.

"There you are!" Mr. Jenkins, their principal, said with relief. He grabbed the boys in a huge hug. "We saw the lean-to and thought it might be you," he said. "Are you okay?"

"We're fine," Mark said. "Half frozen, but fine!" Everyone laughed.

As the group turned to head back, Denny took one last look at their little lean-to. It was almost completely buried in the snow. Another hour and it would never have been seen.

Lost *(cont.)*

Reading Comprehension Questions

After reading the story, answer the questions. Circle the letter before each correct answer.

1. Denny and Mark were rescued because of their—
   a. fire
   b. shouting
   c. flashlights
   d. lean-to

2. The reason Denny and Mark built a tent of branches was—
   a. to protect themselves from the snow.
   b. Mark had always wanted to make one.
   c. to have a dry place to cook their dinner.
   d. they wanted to sleep overnight in the woods.

3. The lesson Denny and Mark probably learned was—
   a. knowing survival skills is a good idea.
   b. being caught in a snowstorm is not so bad.
   c. shouting for help when you're lost is a good idea.
   d. you can always find your way out of the woods.

4. According to this story, a good description of Denny and Mark would be—
   a. cautious
   b. ashamed
   c. disobedient
   d. determined

5. Who first spoke at the beginning of the story?
   a. Mr. Jenkins
   b. Mark
   c. Denny
   d. The boys' teacher

6. The words that show how Mark felt in the lean-to are—
   a. . . . We have to stay put.
   b. . . . I'm not wasting the day inside!.
   c. . . . We're not going to die!.
   d. . . . I don't want to die here.

Grandma's Birthday

It was a beautiful spring day outside. Lauren could see the sunshine out the window as she sat at the piano in the living room practicing her scales. In the kitchen, her mother was starting to make a cake. The next day would be Lauren's grandmother's 60th birthday, and the family was having a big party. Relatives were coming to visit from all over the state. Some were driving several hours. More than one relative would stay overnight in town.

Lauren quit playing and turned around on the piano bench. "Mom?" she called out.

Her mother called back, "Come in the kitchen if you want to talk."

Lauren left the piano and walked to the kitchen. "Are you sure you don't need help making food for tomorrow?" she asked.

Her mother said, "Thank you again for offering, but you have your own work to do. I think it's more important that you practice your piano and then do your homework."

Lauren went back to the piano. She loved to play piano and often would practice for hours. She would lose track of the time when she played. First, she practiced a song by Beethoven. It was a difficult piece, but Lauren enjoyed it. It was very dramatic music.

Then she started practicing a different type of music. She played a song called "The Maple Leaf Rag." This song was happy and a little tricky because it was so fast. Everything called a "rag" was fast. Lauren liked to play "The Maple Leaf Rag" because it reminded her of the way maple leaves could blow around in the wind. It made her think the leaves were enjoying themselves, having a party of their own.

When it started to get late, Lauren closed the lid of the piano. Her mother was still in the kitchen. Lauren said, "Can I help with anything else? Maybe I should change the sheets on the guest bed."

Her mother said, "I took care of that while you were at school today. Maybe you can help tomorrow, but work on your homework for now."

Lauren went down the hall to her room and got out her math homework. As she studied, she could hear her mother running a vacuum cleaner over the floors outside her door.

The next day, Lauren went to school. She kept thinking about the party and about how hard her mother was working to get ready for it. She had asked her mother to save a chore or two for her to do after school because she wanted to help, but Lauren knew her mother wouldn't save a chore. Her mother would have to get everything done before she could relax.

When Lauren got home, the house looked beautiful. There were flowers in the vases and a banner saying "Happy Birthday" was strung across the living room. Aunt Cassie and Uncle Max had brought Grandmother to town. They had driven six hours.

Lauren gave her aunt, uncle, and grandmother each a hug. Then she said, "The house looks wonderful, Mom. But I wish I could have been more help." Her mother gave her a big squeeze around the shoulders and said, "Your job is to play the piano for us! We need a little party music."

Lauren sat at the piano and played "The Maple Leaf Rag." She played other songs too, but she played "The Maple Leaf Rag" more than once. The guests arrived and Lauren played the piano as she watched them out the window, getting out of their cars and then coming to the front door. She thought how like leaves her relatives were, blowing in with the wind on a beautiful day and dancing at their own happy party.

Grandma's Birthday *(cont.)*

After reading the story, answer the questions. Circle the letter before each correct answer.

1. What does Lauren's mother mean when she says, "Your job is to play the piano for us."
   a. She thinks playing the piano is a chore.
   b. Lauren's mother wants Lauren to entertain their guests.
   c. She thinks the maple leaves should be cleaned up.
   d. Lauren's mother thinks their guests will leave if there's no music.

2. In the story, the Beethoven piece that Lauren plays is described as "difficult." What does "difficult" mean in this sentence?
   a. hard to manage
   b. hard to do
   c. controversial
   d. puzzling

3. Why did Lauren lose track of time when she practiced the piano?
   a. Lauren daydreamed about the music while she practiced.
   b. Lauren became bored by practicing so much.
   c. Lauren was more interested in her helping her mother.
   d. Lauren was thinking about the party.

4. Which of these explains why Lauren's mom said to her, "Maybe you can help tomorrow"?
   a. She didn't like the way Lauren did the chores.
   b. She did not want Lauren to be in her way.
   c. She had planned to have Lauren play at the party.
   d. There were some chores that needed to wait until the next day.

5. According to your answer for Number 4, Lauren's mom might have described Lauren as
   a. helpful and talented
   b. eager and athletic
   c. distracted and forgetful
   d. careless and selfish

6. A main point of this story is how thoughtful Lauren is. Choose the best example of this thoughtfulness.
   a. Lauren practiced a song called "The Maple Leaf Rag."
   b. Lauren thought her relatives were like leaves, dancing at the party.
   c. Lauren did her math homework while her mother vacuumed.
   d. Lauren offered to help her mom make the food for the party.

School Reporter

Damaras was in the school cafeteria eating lunch when she spied her friend Anna. "Hey, Anna. Guess what? My article is going to be in the next issue of the school newspaper!"

Anna gave her a big smile. "That's so wonderful. I can't wait to read it."

Damaras was a new reporter on the school paper. For her first assignment she had covered the upcoming school play. Damaras had interviewed both the lead actress and the lead actor. She had researched the history of the play, which had been written by a man from London. She had spoken with the director, Mr. Clausen, who was also a social studies teacher, and she had sat in on rehearsals to see what it was like to be in the play.

Another student, Troy, who was sitting at the same cafeteria table, overheard them. He repeated, "You wrote a story for the paper?"

Damaras nodded. "It will be printed this Thursday. I think it's going to be the lead story!"

Later that day, as Damaras was waiting for her English class to start, another student, Jeff, turned around in his chair and called over, "Hey, Damaras. I heard you wrote the lead story for the next school paper."

Damaras said, "Yes, I did, but how did you know?"

"Troy told me," Jeff replied.

Their teacher, Mr. Kim, overheard them. He looked at Damaras. "You wrote a lead story? That's wonderful, Damaras."

Then the whole class started talking about it. Some students raised their hands and asked how they could be a part of the school newspaper.

Jeff quizzed Damaras, "Are you going to be a reporter when you grow up? Is that your plan?"

Damaras blushed. She was not used to getting so much attention.

On Thursday, when the paper came out, Damaras ran to find a copy of it as soon as she got to school. She went to the classroom that served as the newspaper office. She picked up a copy and looked at the first page. It was not her article at all! Damaras was disappointed that her story was not on the first page. Then she skimmed the rest of the paper and realized her article was not even in the paper at all! "Oh no!" Damaras cried in dismay. "Now everybody will think I wasn't telling the truth!"

She put the newspaper in her book bag and walked to her locker. As she walked, she kept wondering why her article was not in the paper. The newspaper was put together by students with the supervision of an English teacher, Mr. Kline. Damaras started thinking that maybe one of the editors had not liked her story. Maybe Mr. Kline had not thought that her story was well written. Damaras saw her friend Anna down the hall and quickly reversed directions. She did not know what to tell Anna or anybody else if they asked why her story was not in the paper. She dreaded her English class because everyone there thought she was going to be published.

There were still ten minutes before school started, so Damaras sought out Mr. Kline in his classroom. He greeted Damaras warmly. "Ah, one of our fine reporters!" Damaras could not smile back. She was thinking she should offer to quit the school paper, because they did not like her work. Finally, she asked, "Why didn't my story make the paper? I worked really hard to research and write it."

Mr. Kline looked surprised. "Of course it made the paper," he said. "We all loved it. We're running it as the lead story of next week's paper."

Damaras looked confused. "Next week's paper? I thought I submitted it for this week's issue."

Mr. Kline then reminded Damaras that production time for the paper made it necessary to submit articles at least one week before the issue in which they were scheduled to appear. Damaras had been so excited to see her story in the paper, she had confused the publishing schedule!

"Oh no!" Damaras laughed, relieved to hear they liked her work. "Now how will I explain that to everybody?"

School Reporter *(cont.)*

After reading the story, answer the questions. Circle the letter before each correct answer.

1. What does the phrase "She sat in on rehearsals" mean?
    a. Damaras sat on the stage during the rehearsals.
    b. Damaras watched the rehearsals for the play.
    c. Damaras wrote about the play rehearsals.
    d. Damaras tried out for the play during rehearsals.

2. Why did Damaras think that her article would be running in this week's issue of the newspaper?
    a. She knew that she was the best writer in the school.
    b. The school play was going to be over by next week's issue.
    c. New reporters always wrote an article during their first week.
    d. She submitted the article before this week's issue was published.

3. Which of these explains what Mr. Kline probably meant when he said upon seeing Damaras, "Ah, one of our fine reporters!"?
    a. He was complimenting Damaras for writing a good article for the paper.
    b. He was being sarcastic because Damaras had missed the deadline.
    c. He was trying to make Damaras feel good since her article was not in the paper.
    d. He was talking to somebody else who was in the room at the same time.

4. According to your answer for Number 3, how might Mr. Kline describe Damaras?
    a. eager
    b. organized
    c. conceited
    d. careful

5. Part of the humor in this story is the fact that the news of Damaras's newspaper article spreads quickly around the school. Choose the action which best demonstrates this event.
    a. The whole English class talked about being part of the school newspaper.
    b. Damaras interviewed Mr. Clausen, the director of the school play, for her article.
    c. Jeff asked Damaras if she is going to be a newspaper reporter when she grows up.
    d. Jeff heard about Damaras's article from Troy, who overheard Damaras and Anna talking.

6. Which of these sounds most like something that Damaras would do?
    a. Damaras takes credit for the school cafeteria article.
    b. Damaras argues with Mr. Kline for not publishing her article.
    c. Damaras does not confuse the deadlines for the newspaper again.
    d. Damaras writes a story without doing research.

Diving In

Josh stepped to the edge of the platform. As he looked down, he thought the water seemed as though it was a thousand feet below. This was the third time he had come up here, and for the third time he turned around and walked back to the ladder, afraid to make the dive from the high platform. As he turned, Josh could feel the stares from his classmates, friends, and teachers on the back of his head. He knew what they would say when he got down. They would say he'd better make the dive the next time.

Josh wasn't sure there would even be a next time. He was just too scared to dive from that high platform. It wasn't like it was really that important. This was just an intramural diving team that had been put together by the swimming coach at the junior high school. Josh had made good dives at lower levels, he thought. Mr. Barry, the coach, had even said that if he didn't want to dive from that height, he didn't have to.

He wanted to do it, though. He had wanted to feel like a part of the team ever since that first afternoon when he had seen the other swimmers at practice. He enjoyed the water himself, and he was a good swimmer. When the diving team was started, he leaped at the opportunity to join. When tryouts were posted, his name was the first on the list.

Standing on the ground, Josh stared up at that high dive platform that now seemed to be so far above him. He looked around the pool at the other swimmers, who were either waiting at the ladder to try their own dives or talking to Mr. Barry about the one they had just completed. Josh was sure that none of them had a problem looking down at the distant water from high on that platform. He figured that since he had never seen anyone else hesitate, only he was afraid.

Suddenly, Mr. Barry began walking toward him. "How are you doing, Josh?" he asked.

"I'm all right, Mr. Barry. I just got a little scared up there, that's all," Josh said.

"Don't worry about it, Josh. You know, when I was young, I got scared up there too," Mr. Barry said.

"So how did you ever get up the nerve to dive from up there, Mr. Barry?" Josh asked.

"I decided that I had to stop thinking about it. And I figured if I could get myself off the board just once, I would be a lot closer to success. So one day I just climbed up the ladder, ran to the end, closed my eyes, and jumped off the board."

Josh suddenly remembered exactly what it was like to be up there, when it seemed like a thousand feet above the water. Then, almost immediately, he thought about the feeling he would get in his stomach when he actually stepped from the platform, and how the water might look, rushing toward him so fast. He thought about how it might feel like he was flying and the way the air would turn silent as he fell.

Josh took a deep breath, turned around, and started walking back to the ladder that led to the high dive platform. He knew it was something he would have to do. Even if it wasn't today, he would do it someday.

Diving In *(cont.)*

After reading the story, answer the questions. Circle the letter before each correct answer.

1. The author says that Josh was the first name on the tryout list to show that
   a. he was very eager to be on the team.
   b. there were few people on the team.
   c. he was scared to dive.
   d. he was in junior high.

2. Which of these statements is true about the diving team according to the story?
   a. Diving from the high dive was required.
   b. The coach was an Olympic champion.
   c. The team practiced every afternoon.
   d. It was a junior high intramural team.

3. What did Josh do before he walked back to the high dive for his next attempt?
   a. He signed up for tryouts for the diving team.
   b. He watched a teammate dive.
   c. He practiced on a lower diving board.
   d. He spoke with his coach about his fear.

Here is a story about diving. Some words are missing. For Numbers 4 through 6, choose the word that best fills each blank in the paragraph.

Diving is an _(4)_ activity. The sport is a _(5)_ of gymnastic and swimming skills. In the seventeenth century, gymnasts would move their equipment to the beach. The gymnasts would perform their exercises over the water. This _(6)_ activity became the diving that we enjoy today.

4.
   a. enthusiastic
   b. exciting
   c. effective
   d. annoying

5.
   a. definition
   b. combination
   c. congestion
   d. solution

6.
   a. common
   b. reserved
   c. severe
   d. unusual

The Twins' Revolutionary Secret

Harriet trudged through the snow from the hen house. The year 1778 was starting out as "The Year of the Icicle." She had never felt so cold. She thrust one of her bare hands into the egg basket and wrapped her fingers carefully around a fresh, warm egg.

She wished she were home with her parents, but when the British had captured Philadelphia, her parents had sent Harriet and her twin sister, Molly, from the city to live with Great-aunt Anne on her farm. The twins' great-aunt believed that young ladies should spend most of the day doing fancy needlework.

Great-aunt Anne's farm was 20 miles from Philadelphia. Sometimes it was hard to tell whether the farm was in British or American territory. That summer, British troops had marched by in their red coats. They had all looked smart and elegant and prepared. A few weeks before Christmas, American soldiers had marched through. The twins had been shocked, though. The men didn't have matching uniforms. Some of them didn't even have shoes or boots. They had walked barefoot in the snow.

Molly was waiting for Harriet back at the house. "Come see what Great-aunt Anne traded the cattle for!" she cried. Molly led Harriet to the spare room and showed her baskets of yarn rolled into balls. It was an odd thing to trade a few cows for, but Great-aunt Anne was worried that one hungry army or the other would take her livestock. Molly and Harriet were glad the Redcoats could not get food from the farm, but they wished the American soldiers not only had food but warmer clothes as well.

Suddenly, Harriet had an idea. "Just think of all the socks this yarn would make!" she cried.

"And all the mittens and scarves!" Molly added. She looked as though she had already thought of the same plan.

Harriet laughed. "I think it's time we stop practicing fancy stitches and learn how to knit!"

In the following weeks, Great-aunt Anne taught the twins to knit. She was surprised at how slowly they seemed to learn. Whenever she pointed out their uneven stitches, the girls vowed to undo the whole piece and begin from scratch. Indeed, they seemed to knit the same stocking or scarf over and over.

Actually, the girls were trying to knit as many scarves, mittens, and stockings as they could without letting their great-aunt guess what they were doing. They were afraid that she wouldn't approve of using the wool for the American soldiers. So, whenever they finished a piece, they tucked it under the balls of yarn in the spare room. Though the baskets still appeared to hold yarn, they were actually filling up with finished knitting.

The Twins' Revolutionary Secret *(cont.)*

The twins had one problem they could not seem to solve. How were they going to get their handiwork to the soldiers? A snowstorm gave them the answer. In February, a blizzard closed the roads and stranded a wagon and two horsemen near the farm. One of the riders came to the house and spoke to Great-aunt Anne. She was very excited when she told the girls that an important visitor would be staying with them that night. Their guests would include the American hero, General Granger!

Harriet had no idea who this General Granger was, but she decided to ask him to deliver the woolen goods to his troops. The twins knew they could no longer keep their secret from Great-aunt Anne. They found her readying the spare room. When they showed her what they had been up to, their great-aunt was shocked. Just as she began scolding them, their guests arrived.

Harriet suspected that the general had heard some of the argument before he entered the room. She was certain of it when he winked at her.

"So many stockings, mittens, and scarves!" he said. "Can they possibly be for our soldiers?"

Great-aunt Anne's mouth dropped open in disbelief, but she was pleased to have such a great man thinking well of her. "Certainly," she told their guest. "We must all do our part to win freedom from England."

Harriet and Molly smiled at each other. Great-aunt Anne was sure to scold them later for their deception, but now they knew their knitting would help warm the men who had marched by them in the snow. That was surely worth all the scolding in the world.

The Twin's Revolutionary Secret *(cont.)*

After reading the story, answer the questions. Circle the correct letter before each answer.

1. How did the twins hide all of the completed mittens, scarves, and stockings from Great-aunt Anne?
    a. The girls hid their knitting under the chickens in the hen house.
    b. The twins slipped them to the general every time he came to visit.
    c. The girls unraveled their knitting every day and started over.
    d. The twins buried the completed items under the balls of yarn.

2. Which of these explains what Harriet probably meant when she said, "I think it's time we stop practicing fancy stitches"?
    a. They should practice needlework instead.
    b. They should stop trying to knit.
    c. They should make useful items.
    d. They should learn the basics first.

3. For this sentence, choose the word that means that Great-aunt Anne was preparing for the general.

    Great-aunt Anne was _____ the room where the general would be soon staying.
    a. scheduling
    b. building
    c. surveying
    d. readying

4. Why was the year 1778 called "The Year of the Icicle"?
    a. There were more icicles hanging from the rooftops.
    b. It was a very cold winter.
    c. Summertime never came.
    d. Harriet liked how the icicles sparkled in the sunlight.

5. What shocked the twins about the American soldiers?
    a. They were dressed in red coats.
    b. They were mean to everyone.
    c. They marched pass the house.
    d. Many of them did not have shoes or boots.

6. What was the twins' part in winning freedom from England?
    a. They did work for their Great-aunt Anne.
    b. They were well-behaved.
    c. They made mittens, scarves, and stockings for the soldiers.
    d. They were nice to General Granger.

The Youngest Forty-Niner

Polly Sumpter stood at the rail of the deck and looked at the rolling hills of California. Tomorrow her ship would sail through the Golden Gate Strait and land in San Francisco. Her older brother Tim had turned 18 the week their ship sailed around Cape Horn. Yesterday, Tim told her they had traveled 17,000 miles since leaving Boston six months ago. No wonder the men milling around were anxious to leave the ship and head for the California gold fields. Polly, however, wished they could keep sailing around the world. That would mean she would never have to see Aunt Matilda again.

After her parents died in a cholera outbreak, Polly went to live with Aunt Matilda in Boston. The first thing her aunt did was fire her two servant girls and have Polly take over all their chores. Polly was happy when her aunt married a merchant who was sailing to California to open a store. They sent Polly off to the orphanage where her brother Tim lived. Because she could see Tim again, Polly found the orphanage much nicer than working 16 hours a day for Aunt Matilda. Within the year, however, Aunt Matilda sent for both of them.

Polly knew Aunt Matilda would not have sent for them unless she wanted them to work for her without getting paid. Aunt Matilda did not even pay their fare, because her new husband was one of the owners of the ship.

Polly ran her hand along the deck rail. Except for that first week's seasickness, what an adventure the past six months had been! She loved it when the ship stopped for fresh supplies at villages and cities in South America. South of the equator, summer started in December. That meant that she had two summers but no winter in 1849!

Polly patted the purse tied at her waist. Her adventure had taught her how to earn a living. The men heading for California filled the hull of the ship with flour, tobacco, extra boots, and even small iron stoves. Yet most of them had not brought along anything for mending their clothes. Polly's needle and thread kept her busy sewing up shirts and trousers, and the men insisted on paying her for her work. Whenever the ship stopped at a large port, Polly and Tim spent a little of her earnings on buttons, thread, and more mending supplies.

Polly swallowed hard. Tomorrow she would say goodbye to the men who treated her more like a niece than Aunt Matilda ever had. One man had taught her to play his violin. Another had played checkers with her every day. She wrote letters home for some of the men who could not read or write. The first time she tried to refuse money for writing a letter, the miner scolded her.

"In California," the miner told her, "when someone else does our chores, we have more time to find gold!"

The Youngest Forty-Niner *(cont.)*

Tim shouted for her to come join a small group of men. When she joined the circle, the man who had taught her to play the violin stepped forward. He explained that people were afraid there would not be any gold left if they docked in San Francisco, but that if they sailed up the Sacramento River, they would get to the gold fields much sooner.

The men in the circle were members of the investment company that owned the ship. They wanted to sail past San Francisco, but they felt all the owners should agree to the plan. The only owner missing from the circle was Tim and Polly's uncle. Tim was old enough to vote in his place, but Tim said he would only vote if Polly could vote, too.

Polly hesitated. "We scarcely know our aunt's husband," she said.

Tim stood straight. "And it wouldn't be right not to pay him the cost of our fares if we don't go to San Francisco like he expects."

"We'll take up a collection to help you pay him if that means we can get to the gold fields as soon as possible!" one of the miners proposed.

The other miners nodded in agreement with this suggestion.

Tim grinned. "It sounds good to me. What do you say, Polly?"

Polly grinned back. "I say that this makes me the youngest forty-niner!"

The Youngest Forty-Niner *(cont.)*

After reading the story, answer the questions. Circle the letter before each correct answer.

1. Where did Polly's Aunt Matilda live at the beginning of the story?
   a. San Francisco
   b. Boston
   c. Cape Horn
   d. Sacramento

2. Why was Polly relieved to be sent to an orphanage?
   a. Polly would get paid for her work at the orphanage.
   b. Polly hoped that her parents would find her there.
   c. Polly was able to run away from the orphanage.
   d. Polly could see her brother and not work all day.

3. Which of these answer choices sounds most like something Polly would say or do?
   a. Polly would find a way to trick another miner out of his money.
   b. Polly would pout on the deck of the ship, sighing, "I wish we were back in Boston."
   c. Polly would say to her shipmates, "I will miss playing checkers and the violin with you!"
   d. Polly would run to her aunt and give her a big hug because she missed her so much.

4. Which of these best describes what happens in the story?
   a. A young girl fights to become the youngest gold miner.
   b. A brother and sister argue over how to spend their money.
   c. A young orphan travels to California to search for her family.
   d. A young girl traveling to California decides to join gold miners.

5. What was the worst thing about Polly's travels on the ship?
   a. She missed the orphanage.
   b. She wanted to see her aunt in San Francisco.
   c. She was seasick for a week.
   d. She had to mend the sailors' clothes.

6. What does it mean to "take up a collection"?
   a. to ask for donations
   b. to collect souvenirs
   c. to steal money
   d. to buy a ticket

Walden Robert Cassotto

Bobby Darin must have felt as though he belonged everywhere. During his short life, he was a singer, an actor, a songwriter, a television host, and even an aspiring politician. His music career spanned swing, folk, and rock and roll. When he died of heart failure at the age of 37, Darin seemed to be famous for doing just about everything.

Darin was born with the name Walden Robert Cassotto. He changed his name to Bobby Darin when he decided to go into show business. He took his new name from a broken sign on a Chinese restaurant. The letters M-a-n in the word Mandarin had flickered off, and Darin thought the remainder of the sign was a perfect, short, show-business name that people would remember.

He began his career as a songwriter in the early days of rock and roll. In the 1950s, he wrote "Love Me Right" and "Early in the Morning," songs which other artists recorded. Darin also recorded some of his own songs, such as "Splish Splash" and "Dream Lover." These songs showed he was good songwriter, but he was still struggling for fame as an artist.

After he recorded a song in 1959 called "Mack the Knife," however, everything changed. It was a song that Louis Armstrong and Lawrence Welk had recorded before, but Darin's version became the most famous. The song was number one on the pop music charts. It was Darin's first and biggest hit. Darin recorded many other songs, but none were ever as popular as "Mack the Knife."

During the mid 1960s, Darin changed the direction of his career. He began to write and sing folk songs. He recorded versions of "If I Were a Carpenter" and Bob Dylan's "Blowin' in the Wind," which became hits. He also wrote and sang his own songs such as "Long Line Rider" and "Rainin'."

Darin would never have been happy being just a singer, so when he had time during his busy singing and recording career, he pursued acting roles too. He received an Academy Award nomination for his role in the film *Captain Newman, M.D.* He guest-hosted several TV variety shows and even had his own show, called *Dean Martin Presents the Bobby Darin Entertainment Company*, for a short time.

Darin had always known about the heart condition that caused his death. When he died in 1973, it seemed as though he had been on a mission to do as much in his life as he could. He had a variety of friends. During his life, he called Robert F. Kennedy, Martin Luther King, Jr., Gore Vidal, and Liza Minnelli his friends. He once said his goal was to be "accepted universally as an entertainer and human being." Darin may very well have achieved his goal.

Walden Robert Cassotto *(cont.)*

After reading the story, answer the questions. Circle the letter before each correct answer.

1. Robert Walden Cassotto changed his name to Bobby Darin because—
   a. he never liked his last name.
   b. his friends always called him Bobby and said he was "daring."
   c. his agent told him he had to change his name.
   d. he thought it would be a perfect name that people would remember.

2. Which of the following was Darin's first and biggest hit?
   a. "Under the Boardwalk"
   b. "Rainin"
   c. "Mack the Knife"
   d. "If I Were a Carpenter"

3. The main reason Bobby Darin died at a young age was that he—
   a. had a heart condition.
   b. overworked himself.
   c. was in a fatal accident.
   d. suddenly became ill.

4. The most important thing Bobby Darin wanted was to—
   a. have other artists sing the songs he wrote.
   b. be remembered as a good person and a good entertainer.
   c. find a cure for his type of heart condition.
   d. be acknowledged as the best songwriter of the 1950s.

5. The author began this passage with the sentence "Bobby Darin must have felt as though he belonged everywhere" because—
   a. so many different people sang the songs Bobby Darin wrote.
   b. Bobby Darin was well known for musical talents.
   c. Bobby Darin travelled all over the world to share his music.
   d. Bobby Darin was a singer, an actor, a songwriter, a television host, and an aspiring politician.

6. To find the most additional information about Robert Walden Cassotto, you should—
   a. look under the name "Darin" using library resources.
   b. look up the name "Cassotto" in an encyclopedia.
   c. listen to the song "Mack the Knife."
   d. find a book about rock and roll in the bookstore.

Mission to Mars

On July 4, 1997, space exploration took a huge step. On that day, a spacecraft called *Pathfinder* landed on Mars. The National Aeronautics and Space Administration (NASA) sent *Pathfinder* to discover new information about the Red Planet.

The mission was a complete success. After landing, *Pathfinder* sent a small rover, Sojourner, onto the planet's surface. Sojourner explored more than 250 square meters of Mars. Together, *Pathfinder* and Sojourner took more than 16,000 photos of the rocky landscape. Engineers designed Sojourner to last for only seven days, but the little vehicle ran twelve times longer! *Pathfinder* surprised scientists, too. It sent back information for almost three months. That was three times longer than it was built to last.

Because *Pathfinder* and Sojourner ran for so long, scientists got more information than they ever dreamed of getting. For one thing, they discovered that Mars is very sandy. Pictures of sand dunes around the landing site hint that Mars once had water. Scientists know that water means life. Was there ever life on Mars? We don't know yet.

In addition, the *Pathfinder* mission told scientists that Mars is dusty. Huge "dust devils" on Mars spit enormous amounts of dust into the Martian air. *Pathfinder* also recorded frosty Martian temperatures at 200 degrees below zero Fahrenheit. At that temperature, a glass of water would freeze solid in just a few seconds.

In October, scientists lost *Pathfinder's* signal because the spacecraft's battery had run down. They tried to revive the signal but had no luck. The mission officially ended on November 4.

Scientists hope to use the knowledge from these missions to better understand how life on Earth began. They'll also use it to plan future Mars missions.

Mission to Mars *(cont.)*

After reading the story, answer the questions. Circle the letter before each correct answer.

1. What did NASA do to get information about Mars?
    a. NASA sent the spacecraft Sojourner to Mars.
    b. NASA sent engineers on a three-month space mission.
    c. NASA sent the spacecraft *Pathfinder* to Mars.
    d. NASA sent astronauts to run tests for seven days.

2. According to the passage, how much longer did the Sojourner last than expected?
    a. Seven days
    b. Twelve times longer
    c. 250 days
    d. Three times longer

3. What was the main reason NASA considered the *Pathfinder* mission a success?
    a. Scientists found out that Mars is very cold and dusty.
    b. Scientists got more information than they ever dreamed of getting.
    c. Scientists learned that Mars definitely had water at one time.
    d. Scientists found out that there was once life on Mars.

4. This article gives you reason to believe that NASA—
    a. thinks missions to Mars cost more than they are worth.
    b. will not send other missions to Mars.
    c. will be sending future missions to Mars.
    d. has all the information it needs about Mars.

5. You can tell from this passage that—
    a. dust devils on Mars made the photographs hard to see.
    b. Martian temperatures caused *Pathfinder's* battery to fail.
    c. scientists suspect that life on Earth began on Mars.
    d. scientists will look for signs that life existed on Mars.

6. Based on information in this passage, the reader can conclude that—
    a. Sojourner took more photographs than *Pathfinder* did.
    b. scientists will plan a mission to replace the spacecraft's battery.
    c. conditions on Mars are harsher than conditions on Earth.
    d. engineers designed Sojourner to last as long as *Pathfinder*.

Games with a History

Checkers is one of the most popular board games in the world. The oldest form of the game of checkers began in Egypt in 1400 B.C. and was called alquerque. Checkers is related to another ancient game called draughts. International draughts has a 100-square board. English draughts, also known as checkers in the United States, uses a 64-square board. In 1756, William Payne, an English mathematician, wrote the first book in English about checkers. It is not known when checkers was brought to the United States.

Monopoly began as a game called The Landlord Game. The Landlord Game was invented in 1903 by a young Quaker woman named Elizabeth Magie. She wanted to teach people about the evils of landlords, who have an unfair advantage over renters. Charles Darrow redesigned The Landlord Game and sold it to Parker Brothers, a popular game manufacturer. According to Parker Brothers, Darrow was the world's first game designer to become a millionaire.

Monopoly® is the best-selling game in the world. Over 200 million copies in 80 countries and in 26 languages have been sold. A Braille edition of Monopoly was produced in the 1970s. In 1978, a chocolate version of the board game sold for $600. The favorite game piece is the racecar, and the newest game piece is a money sack.

Scrabble® is a very popular game in the United States and Canada. Scrabble appears in one out of three homes in America. It was invented during the Great Depression by Alfred Butts. He called it Crisscross Words.

Although the first attempts to sell Crisscross Words failed, Butts and his partner did not give up. They eventually trademarked the name Scrabble in 1948 and produced the game themselves. By the 1950s, it had become so popular that it had to be rationed in the stores because the small factory could not keep up with customer orders. In 1972, the Selchow and Righter Company, a game distributor, bought the trademark rights to Scrabble. The rest, as they say, is history!

Games with a History *(cont.)*

After reading the story, answer the questions. Circle the letter before each correct answer.

1. According to the article, what is the best-selling game in the world?
    a. draughts
    b. Monopoly®
    c. checkers
    d. Scrabble®

2. The answer to which of these questions would help you understand the history of games?
    a. How were games invented?
    b. Why is Monopoly so popular?
    c. Where was Scrabble invented?
    d. How many people play checkers?

3. This passage is arranged by
    a. newest game to the oldest game
    b. the history of different games
    c. the manufacturers of each game
    d. alphabetical order by inventor

4. For this sentence, choose the word that means that Monopoly is a well-liked game.
    Monopoly is a very _____ game for Parker Brothers, who have sold over 200 million copies of it in 80 countries and 26 languages.
    a. recent
    b. complicated
    c. successful
    d. expensive

5. Which of these best combines the two sentences into one?
    Jacks and dominoes were once popular games.
    Electronic games are more popular today.
    a. Jacks and dominoes were popular, and electronic games are more popular.
    b. Once, jacks and dominoes were games, but today they are electronic games.
    c. Jacks and dominoes were once popular; then electronic games.
    d. Jacks and dominoes were once popular games, but electronic games are more popular today.

6. When Pong® was introduced by Atari in 1977, the machine was big, the animation was slow, and the game was simple. Today, video games are hand held, the action is fast, and the games are complicated.
    a. Some video games seem smarter than humans.
    b. I do not like video games, because I prefer the outdoors.
    c. Video games have improved greatly in the last 25 years.
    d. The invention of video games was a good thing.

Spring Migration

The sun had almost risen when Ainura finished milking the last of the family goats. She looked across the valley at the purple shadows of the distant mountains. Of all the spring campsites her family visited each year, this one had always been her favorite. She felt a little sad whenever they left it. The family was going to move the sheep and goats to new pastures that day. They would soon be busy packing gear and loading it onto the horses. During the spring and summer, Ainura's and the other nomadic families who lived in western Mongolia were always on the move, leading the herds from one field to another in search of fresh grass.

Ainura poured the creamy milk into leather saddlebags. The saddlebags would be put on the backs of the horses while the family traveled. The repeated bouncing motion of the trotting horses would turn the milk into butter. This work-saving idea was just one of the ways her family used their traveling lifestyle to their advantage.

After finishing with the milk, Ainura helped her mother take down the yurt. Yurts are tall, round tents with domed roofs. They are made out of the same kind of felt used to make hats. The felt is formed into large sheets that are tied onto a wooden frame to form the yurt walls and ceiling. Yurts don't have floors, because families build fires inside them to cook. A hole in the roof lets the smoke out. Their fire's ashes were still hot, so Ainura put the teakettle on to boil while they worked.

Ainura and her mother spent a few minutes carrying out the hanging saddlebags from inside the yurt. They didn't use dressers or trunks to store their things because those would be impossible to move. Instead, everything the family owned was stored in saddlebags, which could easily be carried from place to place. When they were in camp, they simply hung the bags on the walls inside the tent. Once they emptied the yurt, Ainura and her mother began untying the felt sheets and taking down the frame.

Ainura's family moved many times throughout the spring and summer, and each family member had many jobs to do on days when they changed camps. Her father and her younger brother, Batyr, were busy that morning rounding up the animals. She could hear Batyr making up songs as he worked. "My home is round my campfire, my country is the grass," he sang. It was a new song, but it expressed many of the old ideas and values of the nomads. Batyr knew this was Ainura's favorite valley, and he often made up songs about it to help her remember what it looked like when they traveled away.

"Ainura," her mother called to her, "can you finish packing the felt bundles? I need to start loading the horses." Ainura nodded and walked to where several large bags of wool were lying. She wet down small bundles of wool and wrapped them in blankets. This was one way they made felt. Normally, the family turned wet wool into felt by beating it for a long time. However, whenever they traveled, they dragged wet bundles of wool behind the horses with long ropes, which achieved the same result.

Her mother had lined up some horses, and Ainura started tying ropes to their packs for dragging the wool bundles. She looked up and saw her father and brother riding toward her with a few more horses. They were almost ready to start moving, but Ainura took a minute to walk to the remnants of the campfire and pour everyone a cup of tea. It would be another year before they returned here, and Ainura decided it was a good time for the family to stop for a moment and share her favorite view.

Spring Migration *(cont.)*

After reading the story, answer the questions. Circle the letter before each correct answer.

1. What does Ainura's brother mean when he says, "My home is round my campfire"?
    a. He is glad that they have found a place to stay.
    b. His job is to tend the fire to warm the family.
    c. He is comfortable living in campsites.
    d. He wants to build a home with a fireplace.

2. Which of these explains what the author means by "her family used their traveling lifestyle to their advantage"?
    a. The family collects artifacts from all over Mongolia.
    b. The family visits many attractions while traveling.
    c. The family takes advantage of fellow nomadic travelers.
    d. The family uses their nomadic lifestyle to make chores easier.

3. For this sentence, choose the word that shows that the animals graze in fields.
    Ainura's family moves often so that their animals have _____ of fresh grass to eat.
    a. pens
    b. stables
    c. arenas
    d. pastures

4. Which of these statements about this nomadic family is true according to information in the story?
    a. Drinking tea celebrates setting up a new camp.
    b. The family stays in one place through the summer in order to plant crops.
    c. The family's tents are made from animal hide.
    d. The family uses horses to move their belongings from camp to camp.

5. Before Ainura takes down the frame of the yurt, she
    a. hears her brother singing.
    b. packs wool to be turned into felt.
    c. loads up the horses with their belongings.
    d. helps her mother untie the felt sheets covering the yurt.

6. What does it mean that the family was nomadic?
    a. They raised goats.
    b. They lived in the mountains.
    c. They moved from place to place.
    d. They liked to camp.

Danger is Their Business

Most animals try to play it safe. They know that there is always another animal that would like to have them for dinner—and not as a guest! So animals find ways to stay one step ahead of their enemies. Some animals, like deer, try to outrun danger. Bigger animals, like moose, rely on their great size and strength for protection. Animals like the grouse, a small woodland bird, have special coloring that makes them difficult to see. There is still one more way that animals can protect themselves. Just like in the old saying "fight fire with fire," some animals find protection by walking right into the jaws of danger.

For example, a little bird called a plover makes a living cleaning the mouths of crocodiles. Small, swimming animals called leeches, which look like snakes with suction cups for heads, swim into crocodiles' mouths and attack their gums. Even though crocodiles are very strong creatures, they are helpless against the leeches. So, the crocodiles let the plovers help them. A crocodile that wants to get the leeches out of its mouth climbs onto dry land and opens its jaws wide. A little plover fearlessly hops into the reptile's mouth and eats the leeches. The crocodile needs the leeches removed, so it doesn't attack the little bird, and the plover gets an easy meal.

Other animals find similar ways to use danger to their advantage. An ocean fish called the clown fish lives inside the poisonous branches of a creature called the sea anemone. The sea anemone looks like a small bush, but its branches are really poisonous tentacles. The anemone uses the tentacles as defense and to trap food. The clown fish is immune to the sea anemone's poison, so it makes its home inside the sea anemone's tentacles. This way, the brightly-colored clown fish doesn't have to hide. No matter how hungry the other fish get, they can't touch the clown fish without getting stung by the sea anemone.

Some insects also survive by living in a dangerous place. One species of mosquito actually lives inside a predator's stomach! The pitcher plant is a meat-eating plant. It uses sweet smells to attract insects. The insects land on the plant and slip down its sides into a long tube. The tube leads to a bowl (the pitcher plant's "stomach") full of liquid that kills and digests the insects. Some types of baby mosquitoes, or larvae, are able to swim freely in this liquid without harm. By living in such a dangerous place, these young mosquitoes stay safe from other hungry insects that might otherwise eat them.

These animals all use danger to their advantage. It just goes to show that jumping out of the frying pan and into the fire is sometimes the best way to survive!

Danger is Their Business *(cont.)*

After reading the story, answer the questions. Circle the letter before each correct answer.

1. The passage is mostly about.
   a. how animals help each other.
   b. using fire to defend yourself against dangerous animals.
   c. why leeches are dangerous.
   d. how some animals survive in dangerous environments.

2. Insects are probably attracted to the pitcher plant because
   a. its leaves rustle and sound like other insects.
   b. they know there are mosquitoes inside.
   c. the color of the plant appeals to them.
   d. they are looking for fragrant nectar.

3. Why can the plover live safely around crocodiles?
   a. The plover is poisonous to the crocodile.
   b. The crocodile needs the plover to get the leeches out of its mouth.
   c. The crocodile depends on the plover to scare off predators.
   d. The plover hides inside the crocodile's mouth.

4. The author links "jumping out of the frying pan and into the fire" to
   a. hitting predators with frying pans.
   b. jumping out of the way of predators.
   c. using danger to avoid dangerous situations.
   d. scaring animals off with fire.

5. In what way is the crocodile helpless?
   a. It cannot protect itself from leeches.
   b. It likes to eat small birds.
   c. It cannot resist the taste of leeches.
   d. It is not very strong.

6. Read the following sentence:
   The clown fish is immune to the sea anemone's poison.
   What does immune to mean?
   a. attracted to
   b. afraid of
   c. unaffected by
   d. unaware of

The History of Pockets

When people put their hands in their pockets, they rarely realize they are using an invention that is only a few hundred years old. For several thousand years, human clothing did not have pockets of any kind. People cut a circle out of cloth or leather and put their money, keys, or other objects in the middle of the circle. Then they gathered up the edges and bunched the circle into a loose bag or purse. They tied a string, usually of leather, around the neck of this purse to keep objects from falling out.

These purses were usually tied onto belts. They dangled by their strings. Thieves would try to cut these strings to steal the purses. Near the end of the 1500s, men began to ask for slits in their trousers exactly where we have side pockets in pants today. A man still tied the strings of his purse to his belt, but then he pushed the purse through the side slit in his trousers. This made it more difficult for a thief to steal the purse.

These purses were also known as pockets even though they were not yet attached to trousers. We don't know who figured out how to sew this pocket into the side seam and make it a permanent part of the trousers. The invention made it easier and quicker to get something from the pocket. No longer did a man have to untie a purse from his belt and then undo the string around it.

Shortly after the pocket became a permanent part of trousers, people began to want pockets in other garments as well. Both women and men asked for them in cloaks and coats. At first, these pockets were attached near the lower hems of long capes and cloaks. A person had to pull up the garment and keep holding it up while reaching into the pocket. This took two hands. Eventually, people asked for pockets at the hip so that it would only take one hand to use the pocket.

Travelers in the days of the first sewn-in pockets had to journey from town to town in horse-drawn carriages. They began to ask for secret pockets so they could hide small valuables from the robbers who often held up coaches. The robbers could not always find a secret pocket sewn inside a piece of clothing. Today, business jackets for both men and women still have these inner pockets to protect valuables.

Modern travelers sometimes still use purses like those of long ago. Today tourists can buy small, flat bags for their passports and money. These are worn around the neck or waist and are kept out of sight, beneath the clothes. Then, even if thieves steal briefcases or women's handbags, tourists will still have the most important papers and emergency money that they kept tucked out of sight.

Three purposes have shaped the history of pockets. The first is safety. To prevent theft, pockets have evolved inside business jackets as secret places for valuables. Pockets also developed because people wanted to reach money, keys, pens, tissues, and other items quickly and easily. The third purpose of pockets was the last one to develop. Only in the last 150 years have people figured out that pockets offer a good way to keep hands warm in cold weather!

The History of Pockets *(cont.)*

After reading the story, answer the questions. Circle the letter before each correct answer.

1. What is this passage mostly about?
   a. how travelers protected valuable papers
   b. how pockets developed over time
   c. how tailors hide pockets in clothing
   d. how people used to carry purses

2. Which of these statements shows that people use purses today in a way similar to how they were used in the past?
   a. They are worn around the neck and are sometimes kept out of sight, beneath the clothes.
   b. The robbers could not always find a secret pocket sewn inside a piece of clothing.
   c. Both women and men asked for them in cloaks and coats.
   d. The third purpose of pockets was the last one to develop.

3. The original pockets were probably sewn near the lower hem of capes and cloaks because
   a. robbers wouldn't think to look there.
   b. this was where valuables would fit.
   c. hems provide extra fabric needed to make a pocket.
   d. this was a convenient place for people to access.

4. Why did people start sewing pockets permanently into trousers?
   a. Permanent pockets allowed people to warm their hands.
   b. The leather used to make purses was hard to find.
   c. This made it easier to get to the pocket without having to unfasten the purse.
   d. It was less expensive to sew the pocket into trousers than to make purses.

5. Why did people begin putting their small purses in side slits in their trousers?
   a. It was harder for the purses to be stolen.
   b. The purses were less likely to be lost.
   c. They didn't like the weight of the purses hanging from their belts.
   d. The purses didn't get in their way.

6. Pockets kept people's belongings safe. What is another reason people liked pockets?
   a. They were fashionable.
   b. They could hold more than purses.
   c. They were easy to make.
   d. They were easier to use.

New Bus Schedule

Attention, Departing Smallville Passengers!

For the next few weeks, all bus service on the Red Line Northbound (Main Smallville Bus Terminal to Richland) will leave at the regularly scheduled time (see below), but it will be delayed between Norfolk and Richland on Monday through Wednesday due to construction on Route 17. Passengers for Richland should plan on arriving one hour later than normal.

To purchase tickets or passes for all bus lines departing Smallville: go to the Main Smallville Bus Terminal on Greisens Ave.; get in the standard ticket line; tell the agent what kind of ticket you want (day, week, month, or year-long pass); pay the agent by cash, check, or credit card; and receive your ticket.

Blue Line Northbound
Main Smallville Terminal to Brownsville

Destination	Arrival Time	Departure Time
Smallville	None	6:00 A.M.
Albany	6:30 A.M.	6:35 A.M.
Jackson	9:15 A.M.	9:20 A.M.
Smithville	11:30 A.M.	11:35 A.M.
Brownsville	4:45 P.M.	None

Red Line Northbound
Main Smallville Terminal to Richland

Destination	Arrival Time	Departure Time
Smallville	None	6:30 A.M.
Valley View	7:15 A.M.	7:20 A.M.
Reading	8:30 A.M.	8:35 A.M.
Norfolk	12:05 P.M.	12:10 P.M.
Richland	3:25 P.M.	None

Green Line Southbound
Main Smallville Terminal to Austin

Destination	Arrival Time	Departure Time
Smallville	None	6:15 A.M.
Woodsen	9:45 A.M.	9:50 A.M.
Quitman	11:35 A.M.	11:40 A.M.
Lake Galena	2:45 P.M.	2:50 P.M.
Austin	5:15 P.M.	None

New Bus Schedule (cont.)

After reading the story, answer the questions. Circle the letter before each correct answer.

1. This schedule was made in order to—
   a. tell how to purchase tickets.
   b. explain the reason for construction on Route 17.
   c. tell people about new routes from Smallville.
   d. warn people about delays on the Richland route.

2. Where should you go to purchase tickets?
   a. Main Smallville Bus Terminal.
   b. Red Line Northbound.
   c. Smallville.
   d. Greisens Avenue.

3. In order to plan for the schedule changes, it is necessary for a Richland passenger to—
   a. be an hour later to Richland than normal.
   b. travel only on Thursday and Friday.
   c. leave later than normal.
   d. leave from Norfolk instead of Smallville.

4. In order to find out about return trips to Smallville, it is necessary to—
   a. look at a different schedule.
   b. go to the terminal you are returning from.
   c. leave the Smallville terminal.
   d. read the rest of the Smallville schedule.

5. You can tell from this schedule that—
   a. the buses always have many passengers.
   b. it is a temporary schedule.
   c. the schedule changes will not be in effect until later.
   d. there is one kind of ticket to purchase.

6. A good addition to this schedule would be—
   a. a picture of the buses.
   b. a table of departure times for buses leaving Richland.
   c. a paragraph about the town of Smallville.
   d. a list of ticket prices.

Summer Swim Schedule

Joe is interested in getting exercise and competing on a team. He reads about events at the community pools and finds the perfect activity.

Swimming Programs

Summer Swim Team

Join a Summer Swim Team and compete with other swimmers! The program is offered at eight different local pools for youths to 17 years old. The season runs June 21–August 21. Practices are daily (Monday through Friday) throughout the summer. There will be three dual meets: July 10, July 24, and August 7. The championship meet is August 21. Cost: $50.00.

Who Qualifies

Summer swim team is open to all swimmers who are 17 or younger and who can:

1. Swim the crawlstroke with side breathing for the length of a 25-yard pool.
2. Swim the backstroke for the length of a 25-yard pool.

Pools & Practice Times

Buckman	2–3 P.M.	Montavilla	8–9 A.M.
Creston	7–9 A.M.	Peninsula	4–7 P.M.
Dishman	8–9 A.M.	Pier	noon–1 P.M.
Grant	8–10 A.M.	Sellwood	7–9 A.M.

Junior Swim Instructor

A two-week session, 20 hours of instruction, two hours per day for children 11–14 years old. Pre-training for youths interested in becoming swim instructors ($45 per session).

Junior Lifeguard

A two-week session, 30 hours of instruction, three hours per day for children 11–14 years old. Pre-training in lifeguarding, CPR, first aid, and customer service ($45 per session).

Junior Lifeguard & Junior Swim Instructor Session Dates

June 28–July 9	August 9–August 20
July 12–July 23	August 23–September 3
July 26–August 6	

Special Offer

Register for both junior swim instructor and junior lifeguard programs in the same session and receive a $15 discount—both programs for $75 instead of $90. That's 50 hours of training for a combined fee of $75.

Register Online

You can now register online! Visit our Web site at http://www.example.com and then click on the button labeled "Find and Request Courses!" You can select an area of town, a specific community center, a program, or search for classes designed for a specific age range. Just visit our Web site, and you're on your way!

Summer Swim Schedule *(cont.)*

After reading the story, answer the questions. Circle the letter before each correct answer.

1. The reason Joe is interested in the swimming program is that he wants to—
    a. learn how to swim.
    b. get exercise and compete on a team.
    c. learn about being a lifeguard.
    d. become a swim instructor.

2. In order to compete on a swim team, you need to be—
    a. able to swim the crawlstroke for the width of the pool.
    b. able to swim the backstroke for 50 yards.
    c. ages 11–14.
    d. age 17 or younger.

3. You will probably need to be tested before participating—
    a. in the online registration.
    b. in the junior lifeguard class.
    c. on the swim team.
    d. in the junior swim instructor class.

4. This passage gives you reason to believe that Joe will probably—
    a. take the junior lifeguard class.
    b. take the junior swim instructor class.
    c. join the swim team.
    d. register online.

5. The reader can conclude from this article that—
    a. lifeguards like to perform CPR.
    b. it is easy to register for programs online.
    c. it is free to join a summer swim team.
    d. the backstroke is hard.

6. The best way to skim this summer swim schedule is to—
    a. go online.
    b. read the items in bold.
    c. read the date and time schedules.
    d. read only the first section.

Tired of breaking your back carrying school books? Tired of ripped homework, crushed lunches and smashed CDs?

We've got the solution!

Try Hippo's Zippered Backpacks.

Only $22

Every Hippo's Zippered Backpack is made with durable, organic denim and double stitched with industrial strength nylon thread. We use heavy-duty double zippers so you can open your Hippo's Zippered Backpack from either side. Our patented quilted Komfort back pads help relieve muscle strain when your teachers give you too much homework—and let's face it, when don't they? A padded CD player holder protects your tunes from the bumps in life. Say "Goodbye!" to strap burn with our reinforced handles and straps. Also, check out our unique side file pockets. Our high-strength mesh pockets use sturdy nylon toggle-pull cords.

Available in Five Bright Colors:

Pretty Pink, Mango Orange, Silly Putty Red, Goldfinch Green, and Mellow Yellow. Also available in basic denim blue for those who like the jeans look from head to toe.

To place an order, click on our Web site http://www.example.com/hippos! Please allow two weeks for delivery.

Hippo's Zippered Backpacks are all the rage!

Try Hippo's Zippered Backpacks *(cont.)*

After reading the story, answer the questions. Circle the letter before each correct answer.

1. In order to purchase a Hippo backpack you need to—
    a. send for an order blank.
    b. go to the store in July or August.
    c. go to the Web site listed in the ad.
    d. ask a parent to take you to the store.

2. Why are the zippered backpacks quilted on the back?
    a. To protect papers and CDs
    b. To help relieve muscle strain
    c. To make them look softer and more comfortable
    d. To protect the backpacks from the rain

3. You can tell that "reinforced" handles and straps are—
    a. attractive handles and straps.
    b. extra long handles and straps.
    c. handles and straps with extra material.
    d. colorful handles and straps.

4. This ad gives you reason to believe that—
    a. the Hippo backpack is made to be very sturdy.
    b. double zippers are used in case one side gets stuck.
    c. the Hippo backpack may not be good for backpacking.
    d. the reader can get the backpack on sale any time.

5. The author begins this ad with some questions because she wants to—
    a. get information from the reader.
    b. express that students carry too many books.
    c. answer questions the company has been asked.
    d. interest the reader in the product.

6. To find out more about Hippo zippered backpacks, you should—
    a. go to a bookstore and find a book about backpacking.
    b. go to the Web site named in the ad.
    c. look up backpacks in a department store catalog.
    d. look at your friend's backpack.

Letter Club

One day, Tasha got some mail from her friend who recently moved to the other side of the country. Tasha loves getting mail and was very excited. When she opened the envelope, she found a short letter and a list of ten names with addresses. It was an invitation to join a letter-sending club.

Dear Friend:

Welcome to the Letter Club! Copies of this letter have been going around the world for many years now. This letter helps inquisitive people find out about other places. By following the steps below, one young girl got letters from all seven continents—even from Antarctica! Be sure to ask your parents for permission before you join the Letter Club. Then send out your letters today! You, too, can learn about places that interest you and that you want to know more about.

What to do:

1. Look at the list of ten names.

2. Send a postcard or letter to the person whose name is at the top of the list.

3. Remove the name of the person you sent a postcard to from the list.

4. Recopy the remaining nine names and addresses and add your own to the bottom.

5. Send a copy of this letter and the new list to ten people you know, but not to anyone on the list.

6. Start checking your mail for exciting postcards and letters!

How it works:

1. The ten people you send this letter and your list to will send a postcard or letter to the person whose name is first on the list.

2. Then, they will remove that name from the list, add their name to the bottom, and send copies of this letter and their new list to ten people they know.

3. After awhile, your name will work its way to the top of the list. When this happens, you will start getting letters from all over world! It usually takes a couple of months before you begin receiving letters.

Because your name will soon appear on so many people's lists, you might receive hundreds of postcards or letters from many different and exciting locations!

Some hints for getting exciting letters:

If you want to get letters from interesting places, try sending this letter and your list to people you know who live far away from you. For example, maybe your grandparents live in another state, or you have a friend who moved out of town. If you try to send this letter and your list as far away as possible, you will be sure to get letters from faraway places, too!

Letter Club *(cont.)*

After reading the story, answer the questions. Circle the letter before each correct answer.

1. In order to get letters from all over the world, the passage suggests that Tasha—
    a. write to a young girl who got letters from all seven continents.
    b. send out letters only to people in her hometown.
    c. send letters to ten of her friends.
    d. write a letter back to her friend.

2. In order to participate in the Letter Club, Tasha should—
    a. find the names of ten people she doesn't know to send letters to.
    b. decide what countries she wants to get mail from.
    c. send a postcard to all the people listed in the letter from her friend.
    d. ask her parents for permission to join the club.

3. When this letter talks about inquisitive people, it means people who are—
    a. unusual
    b. curious
    c. boring
    d. careful

4. According to the letter, copies of the letter—
    a. first came from a girl in Antarctica.
    b. have been going around the world for a long time.
    c. need to go to all seven continents.
    d. should be signed by your parents.

5. In what way does the welcome letter to the Letter Club try to interest the reader in joining?
    a. By telling the reader about other countries
    b. By suggesting the reader might get lots of mail
    c. By indicating that the Letter Club is a new idea
    d. By telling the reader letters will start arriving in a few days

6. As a result of receiving the letter, Tasha will probably—
    a. travel to ten faraway places.
    b. follow the instructions in the letter.
    c. put her name at the top of the list.
    d. return the letter and list to her friend.

Victor Video Game Product Rebate Offer

$3 Rebate on all *Victor Video Games*!

Mail within 30 days of purchase.

Offer expires December 31.

Here's How It Works!

Buy any Victor Video Game, then mail—

1. Completed original rebate certificate (no copies accepted)

2. Original UPC bar code from any Victor Video Game

3. Copy of cash receipt, dated no later than December 31, with Victor Video Game product purchase circled.

All claims must be postmarked by December 31. Requests from groups, post office boxed, or organizations will not be honored. Employees of Victor Video, Inc. are not eligible for this offer.

Offer good only in the U.S. on product(s) noted above. Void where prohibited by law. Please allow 4-6 weeks for delivery. Limit one (1) $3 rebate per address, family, or individual. This offer cannot be combined with any other offer.

Questions? Call toll free 1-800-555-4443.

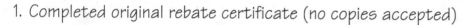

Mail to:
Victor Video Game Rebate
P.O. Box 4443, Dept. 9943
Kalamazoo, MO 49002-4443

You will receive your $3.00 rebate by mail.

Please mail my rebate to:

Name: _____

Address: _____

City: _____

State: _____

Zip Code: _____

Victor Video Game Product
Rebate Offer *(cont.)*

After reading the story, answer the questions. Circle the letter before each correct answer.

1. According to the rebate offer
    a. the purchaser can submit a rebate by phone.
    b. rebates submitted before December 31 are void.
    c. there is a limit of one rebate per address.
    d. an individual can get three rebates.

2. The rebate offer says "Void where prohibited by law." The word *void* means
    a. accepted
    b. promised
    c. allowed
    d. cancelled

3. The rebate offer advises the buyer that
    a. the buyer must call the toll free phone number.
    b. people in Canada should mail their request early.
    c. employees can receive only one rebate per address.
    d. no copies of the certificate will be accepted.

4. If a buyer's information arrived on December 31, when can he or she expect a rebate?
    a. after April
    b. late March
    c. early January
    d. mid-February

5. What is a rebate?
    a. It is a refund if the product doesn't work.
    b. It is like a coupon to use toward the purchase of other products.
    c. It is money given back by the company.
    d. It is a gift certificate.

6. In what country or countries must a person live in order to receive a rebate?
    a. In Canada
    b. In the United States
    c. In any country
    d. Both a and b

> **Directions:** Read this story carefully. When you are completely finished answer the questions on the next page. Make sure to completely fill in the bubbles.

The Mysterious Neighbor

The banging started again that night. Gilbert turned over in bed and looked at the clock on his bedside table. It was after ten. Gilbert listened to the steady beat of sound. The noise had come from the new neighbor's apartment for three nights in a row. What could it be?

Gilbert had seen the new neighbor a few times since he had moved in. The neighbor was an older man who walked with a cane. Gilbert couldn't imagine what he could be doing to make all that noise.

The next night Gilbert was ready. He put a large glass on his bedside table and set his alarm clock for five minutes to ten. After the alarm woke him up, he got dressed and put the mouth of the glass against the wall. Then he put his ear next to the glass to listen. The glass made a natural amplifier. After ten minutes of listening, he hadn't heard anything strange. Then, suddenly, he heard a loud crash and someone shout!

"Oh no," thought Gilbert. He ran out and called for his mom. "Mom, the weird guy next door hurt himself. I heard a big crash through the wall and he was screaming."

"Are you sure?" asked his mom, looking up from the television. Then they heard a knock on the door. Gilbert's mother got up and looked through the peephole. "It looks like our new neighbor," she said and opened the door. "Hi, Mr. Lange. Are you OK? Gilbert here thought he heard some noise in your apartment."

"Sorry to bother you," said the man. "But could you help me for a minute? I've knocked over some lumber, and I need help propping it back up."

At last! thought Gilbert. He would get to see what mystery the man was working on. "I think Gilbert can help you," said his mother. "How's your wife doing?"

"She's much happier since I got the new cabinets installed," said the man cheerfully.

"You have a wife?" asked Gilbert. "How come we never see her?"

"Why don't you come meet her, Gilbert?" asked the man. Gilbert and his mother followed the man to his apartment. Inside, there was an older woman in a wheelchair working in the kitchen. Gilbert noticed that the kitchen counters were very wide and didn't have anything underneath them so the woman could wheel her legs under the counters to reach things she needed.

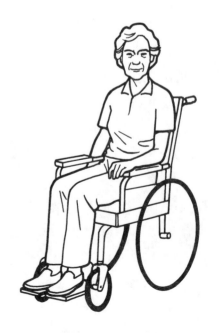

"So that's what you were doing!" said Gilbert. "I heard you building these counters the last couple of nights."

"That's right," said the woman. "My husband spends his days at work or going with me to the clinic. The only time he could build these was at night. Sorry if we bothered you."

"That's all right," said Gilbert. "Maybe I can help you out during the day, now that we're all friends."

The Mysterious Neighbor *(cont.)*

1. Part of the mystery in this story is the use of suspense. Choose the event that is the best example of mystery.
   - (a.) Then, suddenly, he heard a loud crash and someone shout!
   - (b.) Gilbert and his mother followed the man to his apartment.
   - (c.) Gilbert listened to the steady beat of sound.
   - (d.) Then he put his ear next to the glass to listen.

2. In the story, Mr. Lange says, "She's much happier since I got the new cabinets installed." Which of these definitions of installed is Mr. Lange using?
   - (a.) invested in
   - (b.) established
   - (c.) put in
   - (d.) positioned

3. Which of these best describes what happened in the story?
   - (a.) A mother and her son investigate a mystery.
   - (b.) A man teaches a boy how to build cabinets.
   - (c.) A boy is interested in what his neighbor is doing.
   - (d.) A man tries to scare his young neighbor.

4. The answer to which of these questions would help you understand why Mr. Lange is building new cabinets?
   - (a.) When did the Langes move into the apartment?
   - (b.) What does Mr. Lange do for a living?
   - (c.) Where is Mrs. Lange's clinic?
   - (d.) How does Mrs. Lange work in the kitchen?

5. According to the story, Gilbert's glass was a natural amplifier. An *amplifier* is probably a tool that
   - (a.) sees through walls.
   - (b.) makes sounds louder.
   - (c.) quiets loud noises.
   - (d.) locates hidden objects.

6. How did Gilbert react to meeting Mrs. Lange?
   - (a.) He was embarrassed and too shy to talk to her.
   - (b.) He was angry that their noise had kept him awake.
   - (c.) Gilbert was afraid of the mysterious neighbor.
   - (d.) He was glad to know who was living next door.

Directions: Read this story carefully. When you are completely finished answer the questions on the next page. Make sure to completely fill in the bubbles.

The History of the Vacuum Cleaner

Few people today would be willing do what H. Cecil Booth did to invent the first vacuum cleaner. Booth, an Englishman, had seen a suction device that tried to remove dust from a carpet. The machine did not work well. It could only stir the dust into the air. In a few minutes, that dust settled back onto the carpet.

Booth wanted to invent a vacuum device that not only pulled dust from a carpet but also trapped it so that it could not return to the rug. To understand how suction worked, Booth tried a simple experiment. He put his lips against a sofa and tried to suck air from the fabric. Instead, he choked and coughed from all the dust!

Booth decided that the motor of a vacuum machine would be as bothered by the dust as he had been. How could he keep dirt from clogging the motor and shutting it down? He knew this would take a special filter. The filter had to trap the dust and debris while letting the cleaned air pass through the filter's fabric.

Once again Booth experimented. He lay on a rug and sucked air from it through several kinds of cloth. The one that worked best was his handkerchief, made of tightly woven cotton. In 1901, he introduced a bag for suction devices made from that fabric. Booth's vacuum cleaner was as large as a modern refrigerator. It took two people to run it. One had to push the vacuum cleaner around on its wheels. The other person had to work the long, heavy hose.

During the First World War, Booth's machines found a new use. One of London's huge buildings was used to house hundreds of sailors who had spotted fever, a terrible disease. Doctors did not know how to stop the disease from spreading but suspected that the dust in the old building had something to do with the illness.

Over a dozen of Booth's vacuum machines went to work cleaning the big building. They worked for two weeks sucking up the dust and dirt from the floors, ceilings, and walls. When the job was over, workers hauled off twenty-six truckloads of dust and dirt. This debris was buried to keep the germs from spreading. Once all the dust was removed from the building, the spotted fever vanished. Now Booth's machines were seen as more than just cleaning devices. They now became famous as disease fighters.

Though Booth's machines worked well for public buildings, few private homes could afford them. Not only were they expensive to buy, but they required two people to operate them. In America, inventors went to work trying to make Booth's machines smaller and more affordable. When they succeeded in producing the first vacuum cleaner that one person could operate, centuries of cleaning customs changed.

Before the vacuum cleaner, a family had to take all of its rugs, curtains, and cloth-covered furniture outside for cleaning. This was done outdoors so that the dirt and dust would blow away and not settle back onto the furniture and carpeting. The rugs were hung on a clothesline and beaten with bats, brooms, or devices known as carpet whips. Cloth-covered furniture and mattresses were beaten in the same way. The vacuum cleaner allowed people to clean their rugs and furniture without removing them from the home. Now, people can enjoy vacuuming instead of sneezing and coughing from all the dust they have to beat from their furniture and rugs.

The History of the Vacuum Cleaner *(cont.)*

1. The author says that Booth "choked and coughed from all the dust" to show that
   - (a.) there was a lot of dirt hidden in the fabric.
   - (b.) people could get sick from breathing dust.
   - (c.) the current style of vacuum didn't work.
   - (d.) there was a better way to clean furniture.

2. For this sentence, choose the word that means that people's habits changed.

   It became a new _____ to vacuum rugs and furniture instead of beating them.
   - (a.) appliance
   - (b.) product
   - (c.) idea
   - (d.) custom

3. According to the article, what disease was Booth's invention able to fight?
   - (a.) spotted fever
   - (b.) scarlet fever
   - (c.) chicken pox
   - (d.) small pox

4. Why was the dirt that was vacuumed up in the old building buried?
   - (a.) The dust and dirt could be used to help the farmers' crops.
   - (b.) The germs would die if they didn't get sunlight.
   - (c.) The germs in the dust couldn't get stirred up and spread.
   - (d.) The dust would take up too many trash bags.

5. What was the problem with the first suction device?
   - (a.) The dirt settled back on the carpet.
   - (b.) It didn't pick up dirt.
   - (c.) It made people sick.
   - (d.) It was too expensive.

6. What was inconvenient about the first vacuum cleaner?
   - (a.) It was easier to clean the rugs outside.
   - (b.) It took two people to run it.
   - (c.) It was noisy.
   - (d.) It was hard to clean.

Directions: Read this story carefully. When you are completely finished answer the questions on the next page. Make sure to completely fill in the bubbles.

Be Prepared

Jared and Rashid live in a big city, but they both want to explore the outdoors. This summer they decide to take a hiking trip in Secret Valley State Park. They aren't sure what they should pack for their hike, so they call the park ranger. The ranger makes sure that Jared and Rashid understand how important it is to be properly prepared when hiking in the wilderness. The ranger mails them a list of what things they should know and bring to make their hike safe and enjoyable.

What to Bring on a Hike

1. Mess kit—for cooking and eating outdoors
2. Raincoat—or a poncho, in case it rains
3. Backpack—to carry your supplies in
4. Wooden matches—Safely tuck them inside a waterproof container.
5. Canteen with water—to keep you from dehydrating during your hike
6. Sunscreen and hat—Use them for sunburn protection.
7. First-aid kit—a pain reliever, bandages, antibiotic ointment, and snakebite kit
8. Compass—to prevent getting lost on hikes
9. Bug repellent/bug bite treatment—protection from hungry bugs
10. Flashlight and batteries—Make sure you have good batteries!
11. Whistle—In case you get lost, a whistle is a lot easier to hear than a yell.

What to Wear on a Hike

1. Socks—two pairs—one to wear and one as a spare in case your feet get wet
2. Shoes—hiking boots and bring along a pair of sneakers
3. Clothes—sturdy pants or jeans and long-sleeved shirts

Other Things to Know and Do

1. File a hiking plan—In case you get lost, we want to find you quickly!
2. Put a new battery in your watch—A fresh battery will be your best friend.
3. Rest frequently—Be sure to rest at least five minutes each hour so you don't get overtired. Rest before you feel tired and you will get your energy back faster.

Be Prepared *(cont.)*

1. What did Jared and Rashid do to find out about hiking in Secret Valley State Park?
   - (a.) They went to a camping store.
   - (b.) They went to the park ranger office.
   - (c.) They called the park office to find out about different trails.
   - (d.) They called a park ranger.

2. What should you bring to prevent getting lost on a hiking trip?
   - (a.) Wooden matches
   - (b.) A compass
   - (c.) A whistle
   - (d.) A backpack

3. How often should you rest during a hike?
   - (a.) Once a day
   - (b.) Every five minutes
   - (c.) At least five minutes each hour
   - (d.) One hour on the last day of the hike

4. The most important thing the park ranger wants Jared and Rashid to know is—
   - (a.) how to keep rested.
   - (b.) how to make their hike safe and enjoyable.
   - (c.) how to call for help.
   - (d.) what to do to stay warm and dry.

5. Based on information in this passage, the reader can tell that—
   - (a.) Secret Valley State Park is a bug-free area.
   - (b.) preparing for a hiking trip is very simple.
   - (c.) Jared and Rashid will not follow the park ranger's suggestions.
   - (d.) the park ranger has had experience with lost hikers.

6. To find out more about hiking, the best thing to do would be to—
   - (a.) search the Internet for information about hiking.
   - (b.) look in the phone book.
   - (c.) ask your parents.
   - (d.) read the back of a package of trail mix.

Practice Answer Sheet

This sheet may be reproduced and used with the reading comprehension questions. Each box can be used with one story. Using the answer sheets with the stories and questions gives extra practice in test preparation.

Page 5	Page 7	Page 9
1. ⓐ ⓑ ⓒ ⓓ	1. ⓐ ⓑ ⓒ ⓓ	1. ⓐ ⓑ ⓒ ⓓ
2. ⓐ ⓑ ⓒ ⓓ	2. ⓐ ⓑ ⓒ ⓓ	2. ⓐ ⓑ ⓒ ⓓ
3. ⓐ ⓑ ⓒ ⓓ	3. ⓐ ⓑ ⓒ ⓓ	3. ⓐ ⓑ ⓒ ⓓ
4. ⓐ ⓑ ⓒ ⓓ	4. ⓐ ⓑ ⓒ ⓓ	4. ⓐ ⓑ ⓒ ⓓ
5. ⓐ ⓑ ⓒ ⓓ	5. ⓐ ⓑ ⓒ ⓓ	5. ⓐ ⓑ ⓒ ⓓ
6. ⓐ ⓑ ⓒ ⓓ	6. ⓐ ⓑ ⓒ ⓓ	6. ⓐ ⓑ ⓒ ⓓ
Page 11	**Page 14**	**Page 17**
1. ⓐ ⓑ ⓒ ⓓ	1. ⓐ ⓑ ⓒ ⓓ	1. ⓐ ⓑ ⓒ ⓓ
2. ⓐ ⓑ ⓒ ⓓ	2. ⓐ ⓑ ⓒ ⓓ	2. ⓐ ⓑ ⓒ ⓓ
3. ⓐ ⓑ ⓒ ⓓ	3. ⓐ ⓑ ⓒ ⓓ	3. ⓐ ⓑ ⓒ ⓓ
4. ⓐ ⓑ ⓒ ⓓ	4. ⓐ ⓑ ⓒ ⓓ	4. ⓐ ⓑ ⓒ ⓓ
5. ⓐ ⓑ ⓒ ⓓ	5. ⓐ ⓑ ⓒ ⓓ	5. ⓐ ⓑ ⓒ ⓓ
6. ⓐ ⓑ ⓒ ⓓ	6. ⓐ ⓑ ⓒ ⓓ	6. ⓐ ⓑ ⓒ ⓓ
Page 19	**Page 21**	**Page 23**
1. ⓐ ⓑ ⓒ ⓓ	1. ⓐ ⓑ ⓒ ⓓ	1. ⓐ ⓑ ⓒ ⓓ
2. ⓐ ⓑ ⓒ ⓓ	2. ⓐ ⓑ ⓒ ⓓ	2. ⓐ ⓑ ⓒ ⓓ
3. ⓐ ⓑ ⓒ ⓓ	3. ⓐ ⓑ ⓒ ⓓ	3. ⓐ ⓑ ⓒ ⓓ
4. ⓐ ⓑ ⓒ ⓓ	4. ⓐ ⓑ ⓒ ⓓ	4. ⓐ ⓑ ⓒ ⓓ
5. ⓐ ⓑ ⓒ ⓓ	5. ⓐ ⓑ ⓒ ⓓ	5. ⓐ ⓑ ⓒ ⓓ
6. ⓐ ⓑ ⓒ ⓓ	6. ⓐ ⓑ ⓒ ⓓ	6. ⓐ ⓑ ⓒ ⓓ

Practice Answer Sheet *(cont.)*

Page 25	Page 27	Page 29
1. ⓐ ⓑ ⓒ ⓓ	1. ⓐ ⓑ ⓒ ⓓ	1. ⓐ ⓑ ⓒ ⓓ
2. ⓐ ⓑ ⓒ ⓓ	2. ⓐ ⓑ ⓒ ⓓ	2. ⓐ ⓑ ⓒ ⓓ
3. ⓐ ⓑ ⓒ ⓓ	3. ⓐ ⓑ ⓒ ⓓ	3. ⓐ ⓑ ⓒ ⓓ
4. ⓐ ⓑ ⓒ ⓓ	4. ⓐ ⓑ ⓒ ⓓ	4. ⓐ ⓑ ⓒ ⓓ
5. ⓐ ⓑ ⓒ ⓓ	5. ⓐ ⓑ ⓒ ⓓ	5. ⓐ ⓑ ⓒ ⓓ
6. ⓐ ⓑ ⓒ ⓓ	6. ⓐ ⓑ ⓒ ⓓ	6. ⓐ ⓑ ⓒ ⓓ

Page 31	Page 33	Page 35
1. ⓐ ⓑ ⓒ ⓓ	1. ⓐ ⓑ ⓒ ⓓ	1. ⓐ ⓑ ⓒ ⓓ
2. ⓐ ⓑ ⓒ ⓓ	2. ⓐ ⓑ ⓒ ⓓ	2. ⓐ ⓑ ⓒ ⓓ
3. ⓐ ⓑ ⓒ ⓓ	3. ⓐ ⓑ ⓒ ⓓ	3. ⓐ ⓑ ⓒ ⓓ
4. ⓐ ⓑ ⓒ ⓓ	4. ⓐ ⓑ ⓒ ⓓ	4. ⓐ ⓑ ⓒ ⓓ
5. ⓐ ⓑ ⓒ ⓓ	5. ⓐ ⓑ ⓒ ⓓ	5. ⓐ ⓑ ⓒ ⓓ
6. ⓐ ⓑ ⓒ ⓓ	6. ⓐ ⓑ ⓒ ⓓ	6. ⓐ ⓑ ⓒ ⓓ

Page 37	Page 39	
1. ⓐ ⓑ ⓒ ⓓ	1. ⓐ ⓑ ⓒ ⓓ	
2. ⓐ ⓑ ⓒ ⓓ	2. ⓐ ⓑ ⓒ ⓓ	
3. ⓐ ⓑ ⓒ ⓓ	3. ⓐ ⓑ ⓒ ⓓ	
4. ⓐ ⓑ ⓒ ⓓ	4. ⓐ ⓑ ⓒ ⓓ	
5. ⓐ ⓑ ⓒ ⓓ	5. ⓐ ⓑ ⓒ ⓓ	
6. ⓐ ⓑ ⓒ ⓓ	6. ⓐ ⓑ ⓒ ⓓ	

Answer Key

Lost!, page 5
1. d
2. a
3. a
4. d
5. b
6. d

Grandma's Birthday, page 7
1. b
2. b
3. a
4. c
5. a
6. d

School Reporter, page 9
1. b
2. d
3. a
4. a
5. d
6. c

Diving In, page 11
1. a
2. d
3. d
4. b
5. b
6. d

The Twins' Revolutionary Secret, page 14
1. d
2. c
3. d
4. b
5. d
6. c

The Youngest Forty-Niner, page 17
1. b
2. d
3. c
4. d
5. c
6. a

Walden Robert Cassotto, page 19
1. d
2. c
3. a
4. b
5. d
6. a

Mission to Mars, page 21
1. c
2. b
3. b
4. c
5. d
6. c

Games with a History, page 23
1. b
2. a
3. b
4. c
5. d
6. c

Spring Migration, page 25
1. c
2. d
3. d
4. d
5. d/c
6. c

Danger is Their Business, page 27
1. d
2. d
3. b
4. c
5. a
6. c

The History of Pockets, page 29
1. b
2. a
3. c
4. c
5. a
6. d

New Bus Schedule, page 31
1. d
2. a
3. a
4. a
5. b
6. d

Summer Swim Schedule, page 33
1. b
2. d
3. c
4. c
5. b
6. b

Try Hippo's Zippered Backpacks, page 35
1. c
2. b
3. c
4. a
5. d
6. b

Letter Club, page 37
1. c
2. d
3. b
4. b
5. b
6. b

Victor Video Game Product Rebate Offer, page 39
1. c
2. d
3. d
4. d
5. c
6. b

The Mysterious Neighbor, page 41
1. a
2. c
3. c
4. d
5. b
6. d

The History of the Vacuum Cleaner, page 43
1. a
2. d/c
3. a
4. c
5. a
6. b

Be Prepared, page 45
1. d
2. b
3. c
4. b
5. d
6. a